The Palliative Society

Byung-Chul Han

The Palliative Society
Pain Today

Translated by Daniel Steuer

polity

Originally published in German as *Palliativgesellschaft. Schmerz heute* © MSB Matthes & Seitz Berlin Verlagsgesellschaft mbH, Berlin 2020. All rights reserved.

This English edition © 2021 by Polity Press

Reprinted: 2021

Polity Press
65 Bridge Street
Cambridge CB2 1UR, UK

Polity Press
101 Station Landing
Suite 300
Medford, MA 02155, USA

ISBN-13: 978-1-5095-4723-4
ISBN-13: 978-1-5095-4724-1 (paperback)

A catalogue record for this book is available from the British Library.

Typeset in 11.5 on 15 pt Janson Text by
Servis Filmsetting Ltd, Stockport, Cheshire
Printed and bound in the United States by LSC Communications

The publisher has used its best endeavours to ensure that the URLs for external websites referred to in this book are correct and active at the time of going to press. However, the publisher has no responsibility for the websites and can make no guarantee that a site will remain live or that the content is or will remain appropriate.

Every effort has been made to trace all copyright holders, but if any have been overlooked the publisher will be pleased to include any necessary credits in any subsequent reprint or edition.

For further information on Polity, visit our website: politybooks.com

CONTENTS

Algophobia   1
The Compulsion of Happiness   7
Survival   14
The Meaninglessness of Pain   19
The Cunning of Pain   25
Pain as Truth   30
The Poetics of Pain   34
The Dialectic of Pain   38
The Ontology of Pain   42
The Ethics of Pain   50
The Last Man   55

Notes   61
Translator's Notes (*)   69

Of all the corporeal feelings, pain alone is like a navigable river which never dries up and which leads man down to the sea. Pleasure, in contrast, turns out to be a dead end, wherever man tries to follow its lead.

Walter Benjamin*

Algophobia

Tell me your relation to pain, and I will tell you who you are![1]
This line from Ernst Jünger can be applied to society as
a whole. Our relation to pain reveals what kind of society
we are. Pain is a cipher. It contains the key to understand-
ing any society. Every critique of society must therefore
provide a hermeneutics of pain. If pain is left to medicine,
we neglect its character as a sign.

Today, a universal *algophobia* rules: a generalized fear
of pain. The ability to tolerate pain is rapidly diminish-
ing. The consequence of this algophobia is a *permanent
anaesthesia*. All painful conditions are avoided. Even the
pain of love is treated as suspect. This algophobia extends
into society. Less and less space is given to conflicts and
controversies that might prompt painful discussions.
Algophobia also takes hold of politics. The pressure
to conform and to reach consensus intensifies. Politics

accommodates itself to the demands of this palliative zone and loses all vitality. 'There is no alternative': this is a *political analgesia*. The vague 'centre ground' has a palliative effect. Instead of argument and competition over the better ideas, there is a surrender to systemic compulsion. Post-democracy, *palliative democracy*, is spreading. This is why Chantal Mouffe demands an 'agonistic politics' that does not shy away from debate.[2] Palliative politics is incapable of implementing *radical* reforms that might be painful. It prefers quick-acting analgesics, which only mask systemic dysfunctionality and distortion. Palliative politics lacks the *courage to endure pain*. So all we get is more of the same.

Today's algophobia is based on a paradigm shift. We live in a society of positivity that tries to extinguish any form of negativity. Pain is negativity par excellence. This paradigm shift is also present in psychology, where there has been a movement away from a negative 'psychology of suffering' and towards a 'positive psychology' concerned with well-being, happiness and optimism.[3] Negative thoughts are to be avoided. They should immediately be replaced with positive ones. Positive psychology subjects even pain to a logic of performance. For the neoliberal ideology of resilience, traumatic experiences should be seen as catalysts that increase performance. There is even talk of 'post-traumatic growth'.[4] The idea that we should build our resilience in order to increase our psychological strength has turned the human being into a permanently happy subject of performance, a subject as insensitive to pain as it is possible to be.

There is a relationship between the 'Mission Happiness' of positive psychology and the promise that one can live a life of permanent drug-induced well-being. The US opioid crisis is emblematic in this context. This crisis is not just a matter of the greed of pharmaceutical companies. Rather, its foundation is a fateful assumption regarding human existence. Only an ideology of permanent well-being could have brought it about that a medication originally for use in palliative medicine could have been administered on a mass scale to healthy individuals. It is no coincidence that an American expert on pain, David B. Morris, remarked decades ago: 'Americans today probably belong to the first generation on earth that looks at a pain-free life as something like a constitutional right. Pain is a scandal.'[5]

The palliative society and the performance society coincide. Pain is interpreted as a *sign of weakness*. It is something to be hidden or removed through self-optimization. It is not compatible with performance. The *passivity of suffering* has no place in an active society dominated by ability. Today, pain cannot be expressed. It is condemned to be *mute*. The palliative society does not permit pain to be enlivened into a *passion*, to be given a language.

The palliative society is also the society of the *like* [*Gefällt-mir*], increasingly a society characterized by a mania for *liking*. Everything is smoothed out until it becomes agreeable and well-liked. The *like* is the signature, even the *analgesia*, of *the present*. It dominates not only social media but all areas of culture. Nothing is meant to cause pain. Not just art but life itself should be *instagrammable*, that is, free of rough edges, of conflicts or contradictions that could cause pain. What has been forgotten is that *pain purifies*. It has a cathartic effect. The culture of the likeable and the agreeable lacks any opportunities for *catharsis*. We are thus suffocated by the *residues of positivity* which accumulate beneath the surface of the culture of likes.

A report on an auction of modern and contemporary art reads: 'Whether Monet or Koons, whether Modigliani's popular reclining nudes, Picasso's female figures, or Rothko's sublime colour-block paintings – even, at the top end of the market, excessively restored pseudo-Leonardo trophies – apparently all these need to be assignable upon first sight to a (male) artist and to be so likeable as to border on the banal. At least now a female artist has begun to break into this circle: Louise Bourgeois set a new record for a gigantic sculpture – thirty-two million for her work from the nineties, *Spider*. Even a gigantic spider can apparently be more decorative than threatening.'[6] In the works of Ai Weiwei, even morality is presented in such a way as to inspire *likes*. Morality and likeability enter into a happy symbiosis. Dissidence decays into design. Jeff Koons, by contrast, creates *like*-worthy art that is morality-free, and ostentatiously decorative. The only adequate response to his artworks, as he himself states, is 'Wow'.[7]

Art today is vehemently forced into the straitjacket of the *like*. The old masters are not spared by this anaesthetization of art either. They are even linked up with fashion design: 'The exhibition of selected portraits was accompanied by a video demonstrating how well historical paintings by, for instance, Lucas Cranach the Elder or Peter Paul Rubens could be colour matched with contemporary designer clothes. And of course the video did not fail to mention that historical portraits are a precursor of today's selfies.'[8]

The culture of likeability has manifold causes. First of all it follows from the economization and commodification of culture. Cultural products have increasingly become subject to the compulsion of consumption. They have to assume a form that makes them consumable, that is, likeable. This economization of culture runs in parallel with the culturalization of the economy. Consumer goods come to bear a cultural surplus value. They promise cultural and aesthetic experiences. Design therefore becomes more important than use value. The sphere of consumption enters into the artistic sphere. Consumer goods are presented as works of art, and this leads to a mingling of the artistic and consumer spheres which, in turn, means that the arts come to draw upon the aesthetics of consumption. Art becomes likeable. The economization of culture and the culturalization of the economy are mutually reinforcing. The walls between culture and commerce, between art and consumption, between art and advertisement, break down. Artists are forced to become brands. They begin to conform to the market, to be likeable. The culturalization of the economy also affects production. Post-industrial, immaterial production incorporates artistic forms of production. It has to be *creative*. But creativity as an economic strategy only permits *variations of the same*. It does not have access to what is *wholly other*. It lacks the *negativity* of a break which hurts. Pain and commerce are mutually exclusive.

When the cultural sphere was sharply delineated from the sphere of consumption, when it followed its own logic, it was not expected to be likeable. Artists steered clear of commerce. Adorno's catchphrase about art's '[f]oreignness to the world' was still valid.[9] Art that aims to serve human well-being is, accordingly, a contradiction. Art must be able to alienate, irritate, disturb, and, yes, even to be painful. It dwells *somewhere else*. It is *at home in what is foreign*. It is just this foreignness that accounts for the aura of the artwork. Pain is the tear through which the wholly other can enter. It is precisely negativity that enables art to provide a counter-narrative to the dominant order. Likeability, by contrast, perpetuates the same.

'Goosebumps', Adorno says, are 'the first aesthetic image'.[10] They express the dawn of the other. A consciousness that is unable to shudder is a reified consciousness. It is incapable of *experience*, for experience 'is in essence the suffering in which the essential otherness of beings reveals itself in opposition to the tried and usual'.[11] A life that rejects all pain is also reified. Only 'the act of being touched by the other' keeps life alive.[12] Or else it remains a captive in the *hell of the same*.

The Compulsion of Happiness

Pain is a complex cultural structure. Its presence and meaning within society depend on forms of rule. The pre-modern society of torture had an intimate relationship with pain. Its dreams of power were, in fact, filled with cries of pain. Pain served as a means of rule. The grim festival, the cruel rituals of torture, the glamorous staging of pain – they all stabilize the ruling power. Tortured bodies are insignia of power.

In the course of the transition from torture to the disciplinary society, the attitude to pain changed. In *Discipline and Punish*, Foucault points out that the disciplinary society uses pain in more discreet forms, subjecting it to a disciplinary calculation: 'Punishment of a less immediately physical kind, a certain discretion in the art of inflicting pain, a combination of more subtle, more subdued sufferings, deprived of their visible display, should not all this be treated as a special case, an incidental effect of deeper changes? And yet the fact remains that a few decades saw the disappearance of the tortured, dismembered, amputated body, symbolically branded on face or shoulder, exposed alive or dead to public view. The body as the major target of penal repression disappeared.'[1] Tortured bodies are no longer appropriate in a disciplinary society oriented towards industrial production. Disciplinary power manufactures docile bodies as means of production. Pain, too, is integrated into techniques of discipline. The ruling powers continue to maintain a relationship with pain. Through the use of pain, orders and prohibitions are engraved in the mind of the obedient subject, even implanted in its body. In the disciplinary society, pain plays a constructive role. It *forms* the human being into a means of production. But pain is no longer displayed publicly; it is moved to closed disciplinary spaces, such as prisons, military barracks, institutions, factories, or schools.

The disciplinary society has a fundamentally affirmative relationship with pain. Jünger describes discipline as 'the way man maintains contact with pain'.[2] Jünger's 'worker', in particular, is a disciplinary figure. He hardens in his encounters with pain. In the heroic life which 'strives incessantly to stay in contact with pain', one aims at 'hardening oneself like steel'.[3] The 'disciplined face' is 'closed; it possesses clear direction'. But the 'delicate face' of a sensitive individual is 'nervous, pliant, changing, and open to the most diverse kinds of influences and impulses'.[4]

Pain is a necessary element of the heroic picture of the world. In his futurist manifesto 'Counterpain', Aldo

8

Palazzeschi writes: 'The more laughter one can discover in pain, the more profound one is. One cannot laugh truly without having first dug into the depths of human pain.'[5] According to the heroic worldview, life must be arranged in such a way that it is 'armed' against pain. The body, as the place where pain occurs, is subjugated to a higher order: 'Of course, this presupposes a command center, which regards the body as a distant outpost that can be deployed and sacrificed in battle.'[6]

Jünger juxtaposes heroic discipline with the sensitivity of the bourgeois subject, whose body is not an outpost, not a means for a higher purpose. The bourgeois subject's sensitive body is, rather, an end in itself. It has lost the horizon of meaning that made pain appear as something endowed with meaning: 'The secret of modern sensitivity is that it corresponds to a world in which the body is itself the highest value. This observation explains why modern sensitivity relates to pain as a power to be avoided at all cost, because here pain confronts the body not as an outpost but as the main force and essential core of life itself.'[7]

In the post-industrial and post-heroic age, the body is neither outpost nor means of production. Unlike the disciplinary body, the hedonistic body, which likes and enjoys itself without any relation to a higher purpose, develops a hostile attitude towards pain. To the hedonistic body, pain appears wholly senseless and without purpose.

Today's performance subject differs fundamentally from the disciplinary subject. Nor is it a 'worker' in Jünger's sense. In the neoliberal performance society, negativities, such as orders, prohibitions and punishments, give way to positivities, such as motivation, self-optimization

9

and self-realization. Disciplinary spaces are replaced with zones of well-being. Pain loses any connection with power and rule. It is depoliticized, and becomes merely a matter for medicine.

Be happy is the new formula of rule. The positivity of happiness pushes aside the negativity of pain. Happiness is employed as positive emotional capital to ensure that individuals possess a permanent capacity to perform. The neoliberal dispositif of happiness is highly efficient because the principles of self-motivation and self-optimization allow for almost effortless domination. The subjugated are not even aware of their subjugation. They think they are free. They exploit themselves, without the need for any external compulsion, and in doing so they believe that they are realizing themselves. Freedom is not curtailed but exploited. The appeal to '*be free*' produces a compulsion that is far more devastating than the injunction '*be obedient*'.

Within the neoliberal regime, even power appears in a positive form. It becomes *smart*. In contrast to repressive disciplinary power, smart power does not cause pain. *Power becomes altogether decoupled from pain*. It can do without repression. Subjugation takes place through self-optimization and self-realization. Smart power operates in seductive and permissive ways. Because it parades itself as freedom, it is less obvious than repressive disciplinary power. Surveillance also takes on a smart form. We are constantly asked to communicate our needs, wishes and preferences – to tell our life stories. Total communication, total surveillance, pornographic exposure and panoptic surveillance coincide. Freedom and surveillance become indistinguishable.

10

The neoliberal dispositif of happiness distracts us from the actually existing form of domination by forcing us into psychological introspection. It ensures that all are preoccupied with their own psyches rather than interested in critically questioning their social conditions. The suffering society creates is privatized and psychologized. What must be fixed, some would have us believe, are not social but psychological conditions. In fact, the call for psychological optimization is a way of adapting us to the existing form of domination and veiling social ills. Thus, positive psychology marks the *end of revolution*. Instead of revolutionaries we have motivational speakers, who come on the scene in order to ensure that no anger, or even discontent, arises: 'On the eve of the Great Depression, in the highly polarized 1920s, there had been plenty of labor organizers and radical activists around to rail about the excesses of the rich and the misery of the poor. In the twenty-first century, a very different and more numerous breed of ideologues promulgated the opposite message – that all was well with our deeply unequal society and, for those willing to make the effort, about to get much, much better. The motivators and other purveyors of positive thinking had good news for people facing economic ruin from the constant churning of the job market: embrace "change", no matter how terrifying; grasp it as an opportunity.'[8]

In our absolute determination to combat pain we also forget that pain is *socially mediated*. Pain is a reflection of socio-economic distortions which leave psychological as well as physical traces. Analgesics, prescribed by the dozen, mask the social conditions that create the pain in the first place. The strictly medical and pharmacological

11

treatment of pain prevents pain from becoming *eloquent*, even *critical*. It deprives pain of its character as an object, as something social. The palliative society immunizes itself against criticism through medically induced numbness or numbness produced through media consumption. Social media and computer games have an anaesthetic effect. Permanent social anaesthesia prevents insight and reflection; it even represses the *truth*. In *Negative Dialectics*, Adorno writes: 'The need to lend voice to suffering is a condition of all truth. For suffering is objectivity that weighs upon the subject; its most subjective experience is objectively mediated.'[9]

The dispositif of happiness isolates us. It leads to the depoliticization of society and the disappearance of solidarity. Each person has to look after his or her own happiness. Happiness becomes a private matter. Suffering is understood to be the result of personal failure. *Instead of revolution we thus get depression.* Working on our own soul as best we can, we lose sight of the social relations that lead to social malformations. Tortured by fear and anxiety, we blame not society but ourselves. The catalyst for revolution, however, is *shared pain*. The neoliberal dispositif of happiness nips it in the bud. The palliative society *depoliticizes* pain by *medicalizing* and *privatizing* it. The *social dimension of pain* is thus suppressed and repressed. Chronic pain, a *pathological phenomenon of the burnout society*, does not give rise to protest. In the neoliberal society, tiredness is apolitical. It is a *tiredness-of-the-I*, a symptom of the overstretching of the narcissistic subject of performance. Tiredness isolates us instead of binding us together into a *We*. *I-tiredness* must be distinguished from *We-tiredness*, which is the product

12

of a community. *I-tiredness* is the best defence against revolution.

The neoliberal dispositif of happiness reifies happiness. Happiness is not just a collection of positive feelings that promises enhanced performance. It cannot be captured by the logic of optimization. What characterizes happiness is the fact that it is not at one's disposal. Inherent in it is a certain negativity. True happiness is only possible as *fractured*. What stops happiness becoming reified is precisely pain, and pain gives happiness endurance. Pain *bears* happiness. *Painful happiness* is not an oxymoron. Any *intensity* is painful. *Passion* binds pain and happiness together. Deep happiness contains a moment of suffering. Pain and happiness, as Nietzsche says, 'are two siblings and twins who either grow up together or . . . *remain small* together!'[10] Where pain is suppressed, happiness is attenuated, becoming a dull contentment. Those who are unreceptive to pain close themselves off from deep happiness. The one who is open to pain Nietzsche describes as follows: 'The plethora of *kinds* of suffering falls down like an infinite blizzard on such a human being, just as the strongest lightning flashes of pain discharge on him. Only in this condition – always open to pain from all sides and down to the deepest level – can he be open to the subtlest and highest kinds of happiness. . . .'[11]

Survival

The virus is the mirror image of our society. It shows us what kind of society we have. Today, survival has an absolute value, as if we were in a state of permanent war. All the forces of life are used for the prolongation of life. The palliative society turns out to be a society of survival. In the pandemic, the bitter fight for survival is subjected to a viral intensification. The virus enters the palliative zone of well-being and turns it into a quarantine zone in which *life is completely paralysed into survival*. The more life becomes survival, the greater the fear of death. Algophobia is ultimately thanatophobia. The pandemic makes death, which we had carefully repressed and set aside, visible again. The prominence of death in the mass media makes people nervous.

The society of survival has no sense of the *good life*. Even enjoyment is sacrificed in the pursuit of health as an end in itself. Strict smoking bans exemplify this hysterical pursuit of survival. Enjoyment must give way to survival. Everywhere, the prolongation of life at any cost is the preeminent value, in comparison to which all others must take second place. We are prepared to sacrifice everything that makes life worth living for the sake of survival. In the face of the pandemic, even the restriction of fundamental rights has been accepted without so much as a question being asked. We comply willingly with the state of exception that reduces life to bare life. In the viral state of exception, we voluntarily lock ourselves in quarantine. Quarantine is a viral variant of the camp in which bare life reigns.[1] In the pandemic, the neoliberal labour camp is called the 'home office'. The only difference between the home office and the labour camps of despotic regimes is that, in the former, the ideology of health and the paradoxical freedom of self-exploitation reign.

Because of the pandemic, the society of survival has prohibited church services, even at Easter. Priests, too, practise 'social distancing' and wear protective masks. They sacrifice faith entirely to survival. Neighbourly love is expressed, paradoxically, by keeping one's distance from one's neighbour, who is a potential carrier of the virus. Virology deprives theology of its power. Everyone is listening to the virologists, who have acquired absolute authority in interpreting the situation. The narrative of resurrection has completely given way to the ideology of health and survival. Faced with the virus, faith degenerates into farce. It is replaced with intensive care units and respirators. The dead are counted daily. Death reigns supreme over life, drains it, and thus turns it into survival.

The mania for survival makes life radically transient.

Life is reduced to a biological process that must be optimized. It loses any *meta-physical* dimension. Self-tracking acquires the status of a cult. Digital hypochondria, constant self-measurement with the aid of health and fitness apps, degrades life into a mere *function*. Life is divested of any narrative that could give it meaning. Life is no longer a matter of what can be *recounted* but a matter of what can be *counted, measured*. Life becomes bare, even obscene. There is nothing that promises to endure. All those symbols, narratives, and rituals that made life something more than mere survival have faded into oblivion. Cultural practices such as the worship of ancestors gave vitality even to the dead. Life and death were combined in symbolic exchange. Because we have completely lost those life-stabilizing cultural practices, the mania for survival reigns. Today, we find it particularly difficult to die, for it is no longer possible to find a way of bringing life to a meaningful closure. Life ends in non-time. Whoever cannot die at the right time must perish in non-time.* We age without becoming *old*.

Capitalism lacks a narrative of the good life. It elevates survival to an absolute value. Capitalism is nourished by the unconscious thought that more capital means less death. Capital is accumulated against death. It is imagined as a *capacity* [*Vermögen**] for survival.[2] Because life is finite, we accumulate capital time. The pandemic is a shock to capitalism, but it has not suspended it. It does not provide a narrative to counter that of capitalism. There will not have been a viral revolution. Capitalist production has not been decelerated; it has been forced to stop. There has been a nervous pause. The lockdown has not brought about leisure but enforced inactivity. It has not provided space for *lingering*. It is not true that the pandemic has meant health being prioritized over the economy. The entire economy of growth and performance itself aims at survival.

The fight for survival must be juxtaposed with an interest in the *good life*. A society that is gripped by the mania for survival is a society of the undead. We are too alive to die, and too dead to live. Our overriding concern with survival we have in common with the virus, this undead being which only proliferates, that is, survives without actually living.

The palliative society is a society of positivity. It is characterized by an *unlimited permissiveness*. Diversity, community and sharing are its catchwords. The *other*, as the *enemy*, is made to disappear. The accelerating circulation of information and capital reaches terminal velocity when there is no longer any immunological resistance from the other. Transitions thus become mere passages. Boundaries are removed. Thresholds are torn down. The immunological resistance to the other is radically weakened.

The immunologically organized society is surrounded by fences and walls, as in the time of the Cold War. Space is divided into *blocs* that are separated from each other. But such immunological barriers slow down the circulation of commodities and capital. Globalization, which was given a massive boost following the end of the Cold War, is a process of de-immunization which dismantles all barriers in order to accelerate the flow of commodities and capital. The immunological effect of the negativity of the enemy has no place in the constitution of the neoliberal performance society. In this society, war is waged first of all against oneself. Exploitation by others gives way to self-exploitation.

The appearance of the virus has triggered an immunological crisis. It has intruded into an immunologically weakened, permissive society, causing a shock-induced paralysis. In a panic, borders are closed again. Spaces are separated off from each other. Movement and contact are radically limited. The whole society returns to *the mode of immunological defence*. What we are witnessing is the *return of the enemy*. We are waging war against the virus, the invisible enemy.

The effects of the pandemic are similar to those of terrorism: terrorism also triggers an overwhelming immune response by throwing naked death at bare life. At airports everyone is treated like a potential terrorist. At airports we endure, without protest, the most humiliating security measures. We allow ourselves to be frisked for concealed weapons. The virus is a terror in the air. Everyone is suspected of being a potential carrier of the virus, and this leads to a quarantine society, which, in turn, will lead to a biopolitical surveillance regime. The pandemic does not promise a different form of life. In the war against the virus, life is more than ever a matter of mere survival. The virus only intensifies our mania for survival.

The Meaninglessness of Pain

A chief characteristic of the contemporary experience of pain is that it is perceived as meaningless. We no longer possess a meaningful context within which to find support and orientation when faced with pain. We have completely lost the *art of suffering pain*. Medicalization and pharmacology destroy all 'cultural programs for dealing with pain'.[1] Pain has become a meaningless evil that must be fought with analgesia. As purely physical agony, it lies completely outside the *symbolic order*.

Paul Valéry's Monsieur Teste represents the modern, sensitive bourgeois subject who experiences pain as meaningless, as purely physical agony. He has completely lost the Christian narrative which once served as a kind of divine narcotic or stimulant. 'Pain has no meaning.'[2] With this short sentence, Valéry expresses an unbearable thought that weighs on us as heavily as the death of God.

19

The human being has lost a narrative protection, and thus also the ability to alleviate pain symbolically. Without this protection, we are at the mercy of a naked body deprived of meaning and language: 'This terse sentence marks the historical endpoint of a development during which pain was removed from its cultural codification. For the first time, pain presents itself as something that resists meaning It was only possible to formulate such a sentence after an enormous amount of demolition work had already taken place. In the course of the nineteenth century, physiologists and anatomists seem to have removed Christian semantics from the cultural body for good. Valéry's sentence belongs to the vicinity of Nietzsche's catchphrase "God is dead." With these sentences, the coldness of the cosmos penetrates our bones.'[3]

For Monsieur Teste, pain cannot be narrated. It destroys language. Where the pain begins, his sentences break off. Its existence is registered only by the ellipses: "'Ah-h-h!" He was in pain. . . . "It's nothing . . . much," he said. . . . "Wait. . . . I count grains of sand . . . and so long as I can see them . . . my increasing pain forces me to notice it. I think about it! Waiting only to hear my cry . . . and the moment I hear it, the object, the terrible object, smaller and still smaller, vanishes from my inner sight . . .".'[4]

Confronted with pain, Monsieur Teste falls silent. Pain robs him of his language. It destroys his world, traps him in his mute body. The Christian mystic Teresa of Ávila might be presented as a counter-image to Monsieur Teste. For her, pain is highly articulate. It is with pain that narration begins. The Christian narrative gives pain a language. It also transforms her body into a stage. Pain deepens the relationship with God; it creates intimacy, intensity. It is even an erotic process. A holy eroticism transforms pain into lust: 'I saw in his [the angel's] hands a large golden dart and at the end of the iron tip there appeared to be a little fire. It seemed to me this angel plunged the dart several times into my heart and that it reached deep within me. When he drew it out, I thought he was carrying off with him the deepest part of me; and he left me all on fire with great love of God. The pain was so great that it made me moan, and the sweetness this greatest pain caused me was so superabundant that there is no desire capable of taking it away; nor is the soul content with less than God. The pain is not bodily but spiritual, although the body doesn't fail to share in some of it, and even a great deal.'[5]

According to Freud, pain is a symptom that points to a block in someone's personal story. Because of this block, the patient is not able to continue his or her story. Psychogenic pain is an expression of buried, repressed words. The word becomes *thing-like*. The therapy consists in the liberation of the person from this linguistic block, a liberation that makes the person's story fluid again. Monsieur Teste's pain is a *'thing'*, a 'terrible *object'* that escapes narration.* Without a past or future, it rests in the mute present of the body: 'When the pain suddenly invades, it does not illuminate a past: it only illuminates the present areas of the body. It causes a local echo . . . It thus reduces consciousness to a brief present, to a constricted moment deprived of its future horizon . . . Here we are as far away from any kind of history as it is possible to be. . . .'[6]

Pain has now become *reified* into a purely bodily agony.

21

The meaninglessness of pain cannot be understood as straightforwardly emancipatory, as, for instance, freeing pain from theological pressure. Rather, the meaninglessness of pain points to the fact that our life – having been reduced to a biological process – is *itself empty of meaning*. Meaningful pain requires a narrative which situates life within a meaningful horizon. Meaningless pain is only possible within a bare life empty of meaning – within a life that *no longer narrates*.

In *Thought Figures*, Benjamin talks about those healing hands whose unusual movements give the impression of *telling a story*. Stories are the source of a healing power: 'The child is sick. His mother puts him to bed and sits down beside him. And then she begins to tell him stories.'[7] Benjamin believes that the story a sick patient confides to the doctor at the beginning of treatment is already the beginning of the healing process. He asks 'whether every illness might be cured if it could only float along the river of narrative – until it reached the mouth. If we reflect that pain is a dam that offers resistance to the current of narrative, it is evident that the dam will be pierced when the gradient is steep enough for everything that crosses its path to be swept into an ocean of blissful oblivion. Stroking marks out a bed for this torrent.'[8] The hand of the mother who strokes the sick child creates a channel in which the current of narrative can flow. But pain is not simply a dam that offers resistance to this narrative flow. Rather, it is pain itself that allows the current to flow, so that it might carry the pain along with it. *Pain initiates the narrative in the first place.* Only then can pain be 'a navigable river which never dries up and which leads man down to the sea'.[9]

We live in a post-narrative age. Our lives are determined not by recounting but by counting. Narration is that *mental* faculty [Vermögen des *Geistes*] which can overcome the contingency of the body. Benjamin's suggestion that narration may be able to heal any illness is therefore not far-fetched. Shamans also drive out illness and pain with magical incantations that have a narrative character. Where the mind retreats, the body is empowered. Faced with the intensity of a pain that has become meaningless, the mind has no other option but to acknowledge its impotence: 'Teste's question – "What is a man's potential?" – is a challenge that touches upon man's *maximum* capabilities. But we also need to consider a *minimum*: if sensibility "exceeds any answer", if the "untamed part of the organism" gains the upper hand, the faculty of man is pushed aside by the "potential for pain". Whether shallow or deep, what Valéry rediscovers again and again is the *threshold* where the body that has been left alone on the stage allows the mind just enough illumination for it to recognize its own defeat.'[10]

Monsieur Teste anticipates the hypersensitive late-modern man who suffers meaningless pain. The threshold of pain at which the mind admits its impotence is today lowering rapidly. The *mind* as a narrative faculty is abolishing itself. In modern life, in particular, where our environments cause us less and less pain, the part of our nervous system that registers pain seems to become increasingly sensitive. A hypersensitivity develops. Algophobia, in particular, makes us extremely sensitive to pain. It can even induce pain. The docile body, which has to cope with a great deal of externally caused pain, is less sensitive. And it is characterized by an altogether different intentionality; it is concerned not with itself but rather with the outside. Our attention, by contrast, is more intensely directed at our own bodies. Like Monsieur Teste, we listen obsessively to our bodies. This *narcissistic, hypochondriac introspection* probably has something to do with our hypersensitivity.

Hans Christian Andersen's fairy tale *The Princess and the Pea* can be read as an allegory of the hypersensitivity of the late-modern subject. The pea underneath the mattress causes the future princess so much pain that she has a sleepless night. Many people today are probably ill with 'princess-and-the-pea syndrome'.[11] The paradox of the syndrome is that our increasing suffering is the result of fewer and fewer causes. Pain is a subjective sensation, not something that can be measured objectively. Our increasing expectations regarding the power of medicine, coupled with the meaninglessness of pain, make even minor pain seem unbearable. And we lack networks of meaning, narration, and higher authorities and purposes that could capture our pain and make it bearable. Once the pea is taken away, the mattress will begin to chafe. What is painful, after all, is the persisting meaninglessness of life itself.

The Cunning of Pain

It is highly likely that pain will never disappear. What changes is just the way in which it appears. For Jünger, pain is one of those elementary forces that we cannot make go away. He compares modern man to Sinbad the Sailor. Sinbad strolls around on an island and feasts with his comrades, but the island turns out to be the back of a colossal whale. Irritated by the fires that have been started on its back, it plunges into the depths, and Sinbad is thrown into the sea. 'We find ourselves', Jünger writes, 'in a situation of wanderers traipsing along endlessly over a frozen lake, whose surface begins to break up into great sheets of ice due to a change in climate'.[1] Pain is that element which glimmers through the cracks in the ice. The false sense of security we have results from the fact 'that pain is marginalized in favor of a run-of-the-mill complacency'.[2] But with every raising of the wall that protects man against the elementary forces, the threat also grows.

The pandemic demonstrates that the wall sheltering us from the elementary forces can break at any time. As the palaeontologist Andrew H. Knoll puts it, human beings and the other animals are 'evolution's icing', and 'the bacteria are the cake'.[3] Microbes threaten to break through the fragile surface, even to conquer it, at any time. Sinbad the Sailor, walking about on the back of a whale in the belief that it is a safe island, may be the enduring metaphor for mankind's ignorance. We take ourselves to be safe, but it is only ever a matter of time before we are pulled into the abyss by the elements. In the Anthropocene, humans are more vulnerable than ever. Our violence towards nature returns and exerts itself upon us with even more force.

Jünger believes that pain cannot be made to disappear. He speaks of an economy of pain. If it is suppressed, it invisibly 'amasses as hidden capital accruing compound interest'.[4] With Hegel's cunning of reason in mind Jünger postulates a 'cunning of pain', according to which pain breaches artificial barriers, permeating life drop by drop: 'No claim, however, is more certain than the one pain has on life. Where people are spared pain, social stability is produced according to the laws of a very specific economy, and, by a turn of phrase, one can speak of a "cunning of pain" that never fails to reach its aim. At the sight of this state of widespread comfort, one is prompted to ask immediately where the burden is borne. As a rule one will not have to go far to uncover the pain. Indeed, even the individual is not fully free from pain in this joyful state of security. The artificial check on the elementary forces might be able to prevent violent clashes and to ward off shadows, but it cannot stop the dispersed light with which pain permeates life. The vessel, sealed off from pain's full flow, is filled drop by drop. Boredom is nothing other than the dissolution of pain in time.'[5]

Jünger's postulate of the cunning of pain is not altogether implausible. Pain, it seems, cannot be expelled from life. It seems to make its claim on life felt in all sorts of ways: despite the huge progress that has been made in the development of analgesic medications, there is no less pain. Even the greatest arsenal of medication cannot defeat it. The shadows, as Jünger says, may be warded off, but the room is instead filled with dispersed light. Watered down, pain is broadly disseminated. Today's epidemic of chronic pain seems to confirm Jünger's thesis. In the pain-averse palliative society, in particular, the *silent* forms of pain that have been pushed to the margins grow, and their meaninglessness, muteness and imagelessness persist.

Pain is based on different forms of violence. Repression, for instance, is a *violence of negativity*. It is inflicted by others. But violence not only comes from others. The excess of positivity that is expressed as over-performance, over-communication and over-excitability is also violence. The *violence of positivity* leads to the pain of stress. The psychological tensions that are characteristic of the neoliberal performance society are particularly algogenic. They exhibit auto-aggressive characteristics. The performance subject is violent towards itself. It exploits itself voluntarily until it breaks down. The slave takes the whip out of the master's hand and whips himself in order to become master, to become free. The performance subject wages war against itself. The *internal pressures* this creates plunge the subject into depression. They also cause chronic pain.

We are witnessing a steep increase in self-harming behaviour. 'Cutting' is developing into a pandemic. Images of deep wounds from self-cutting circulate on social media. These are new images of pain, and they suggest a society that is dominated by narcissism, in which all are unbearably burdened by themselves. Cutting is a futile attempt to cast off this ego burden, to break out of oneself, to free oneself from destructive internal tension. The image of the self-cutting victim is the *bloody obverse of the selfie*.

Viktor von Weizsäcker describes the primordial scene of healing as follows: 'When a sister, still very young herself, sees her little brother in pain, she senses what to do before knowing anything: her hand finds its way; she wants to caress him where it hurts – *thus, the little Samaritan becomes the first doctor*. A pre-knowledge about a primal effect is unconsciously at work in her. That knowledge guides her urge towards her hand and leads the hand to perform the soothing caress. For that is what the brother will experience; the hand will soothe him. Between himself and the pain slips the sensation of being touched by the sisterly hand, and the pain retreats before this new sensation.'[6] We are currently moving further and further away from this primordial scene of healing. The experience of healing care in the form of the sensation of *being touched and addressed* is becoming increasingly rare. We are living in a society in which people are increasingly lonely and isolated. Narcissism and egotism are intensifying. Growing competitiveness and the weakening of

28

solidarity and empathy also contribute to people's isolation. Loneliness and the lack of a sense of closeness to others amplify pain. Perhaps chronic pain and self-cutting are also the body's cries for attention and closeness, even for love – telling indications of the fact that, today, there is rarely any *touching*. We seem to miss the healing *hand of the other*. No amount of analgesia can compensate for the loss of that primordial scene of healing.

The aetiologies of chronic pain are diverse. Distortion, strain and tension within the social fabric can cause or intensify chronic pain. In particular, what makes chronic pain so unbearable in today's society is the vacuum of meaning. Chronic pain reflects the fact that our society is devoid of meaning, our *time without narration*. It is a time in which life has become bare survival. More analgesia or further psychological research can do little about it. These only blind us to the socio-cultural causes of pain.

Pain as Truth

In his essay 'Die Schmerzen' [Pain], Viktor von Weizsäcker calls pain the 'incarnation of a truth'. When a separation hurts, the relationship is revealed to have been a true relationship. Only truth hurts. *Everything that is true is painful.* The palliative society is a society without truth, a hell of the same. The 'fabric of life structures' is only revealed 'along pain, as Ariadne's thread'.[1] The structure of life is a 'structure of pain'. Pain is a reliable criterion of truth, an 'instrument for distinguishing between the genuine and the fake among the phenomena of life'.[2] Pain only occurs where a genuine form of belonging comes under threat. Without pain, we are therefore blind, incapable of establishing truth and knowledge: 'Where these separations hurt, there the relationships had been genuine and had become incarnated. And where a human being can suffer pain, there he is really present – there, whether he is aware of it or not, he has also loved. A view of the world's structure thus opens up: where some being is capable of pain, there it is truly integrated, and part of not only a mechanical and spatial side-by-side, but of a real, that is, living togetherness.'[3] Without pain, we have neither loved nor lived. We have sacrificed life for the sake of a *comfortable survival*. Only a living relationship, a true togetherness, is capable of pain. A lifeless, functional side-by-side, by contrast, does not feel any pain, even as it falls apart. What distinguishes living togetherness from the dead side-by-side is pain.

Pain is attachment. Someone who rejects all pain is incapable of attachment. Today, intense, potentially painful relationships are avoided. Everything takes place in a comfortable palliative zone. In his book *In Praise of Love*, Alain Badiou quotes one dating site's slogan: 'Get perfect love without suffering!'[4] The *other as pain* disappears. Love as consumption, which reifies the other into a sex object, does not hurt. It is the opposite of Eros, of *desiring the other*.

Pain is difference. It articulates life. The bodily organs are only known through the specific tone of pain associated with them. Pain marks borders, accentuates differences. Without pain, the body, as well as the world, sinks into in-difference. In response to the question 'Where, then, does pain lead us?', von Weizsäcker writes: 'Firstly, it makes me see that I can only know through pain all the things that are mine. That my toe, my foot, my thighs, and everything between the ground on which I stand and the hair on my head, that all this *is mine*, I learn through pain. And it is also through pain that I learn that bones, lungs, the heart and the marrow are where they are. Each of them has its own language of pain, speaks its own "organ dialect". I might have noticed that I have all these things in other ways as well, but only pain tells me how dear they are to me. The price and value of each one of them I only learn through pain, and in the same way this law of pain rules in the world, determining the price of the world and the things in it for me.'[5] Without pain there can be no distinction, and so no appreciation. A world without pain is a hell of the same [Hölle des Gleichen], where in-difference [Gleich-Gültigkeit] rules, where the *incomparable* [das *Unvergleichbare*] disappears.

Pain is reality. It evokes reality. We perceive reality first of all in the form of a painful resistance. The powerful anaesthesia of the palliative society makes the world unreal. Digitalization also increasingly reduces resistance, makes antagonistic opposition, the *anti*, the *anti-bodies*, disappear.* The ubiquity of the *like* leads to a numbness that undermines reality. *Digitalization is anaesthetization*.

The post-factual age of fake news and deepfakes leads to an *apathy towards reality*, even an *anaesthesia* that protects us *against reality*. It is only when a painful *shock of reality* strikes us that we are able to emerge from this anaesthesia. The panicked response to the virus may be explained in part with reference to such a shock. *The virus re-establishes reality*. In the form of this *viral anti-body*, reality is back.

Pain intensifies self-perception. It *provides an outline* of the self; it draws its *contours*. The increasing incidence of self-harming behaviour can be understood as the result of desperate attempts by narcissistic, depressive selves to re-assure themselves of themselves, *to feel themselves*. I feel pain, therefore I am. We also owe to pain the feeling of our

32

existence. If pain is removed altogether, we search for a substitute. Artificial pain offers relief. Extreme sports and risk-taking behaviour are attempts at reassuring oneself of one's own existence. Paradoxically, then, the palliative society produces *extremists*. In the absence of a *culture* of pain there emerges a barbarism: 'Increasingly stronger stimuli are needed to provide people in an anesthetic society with any sense of being alive. Drugs, violence, and horror turn into increasingly powerful stimuli that can still elicit an experience of self.'[6]

The Poetics of Pain

Writing, Franz Kafka told Max Brod in a letter, was a 'sweet, wonderful reward' for the fact that he was 'pinched, beaten, and ground nearly to dust by the devil'. It was a reward for unbearable suffering. There is a kind of writing that takes place 'in the light of the sun', Kafka wrote, but he himself owed his writing to the 'dark violence' that nearly destroyed his life: he wrote when fear did not permit him to sleep. Without writing, life would end in 'madness'.[1]

Proust was another author who cultivated suffering for the sake of writing. From childhood onwards, his life was marked by illness. Severe asthma attacks tortured him all his life. A few years before his death, Proust wrote in a letter: 'Although I am bitter about the fact that I suffer such unbearable physical pain, which particularly in recent months has been the constant companion of my sorrow, I am attached to them, my sufferings, and I hate the thought they might leave me.' Pain guides Proust's pen. He wrests even language, even *form*, from death. He makes death serve his writing. Without pain, this *passion of writing* would be inconceivable: 'He analysed his own condition, remaining alert, heroically, until the final hour, and these notes and last corrections to the proofs were meant to make the death of his hero, Bergotte, even more vivid, more truthful on the page, were an attempt to present the most intimate details, the last ones the poet could know, the ones only the dying know. . . . In this way, he slaps death in the face: a final, wonderful gesture from the artist who conquers the fear of death by listening to the process of dying.'[2]

Schubert was also a *homo doloris*. *Winter Journey* was born out of pain. Written into his late works is the unbearable pain he suffered, among others that arising from syphilis. The indescribably painful mercury therapy he was prescribed was sheer torture. The mercury was swallowed, and the whole body rubbed with it. The patient had to stay for days in a hot room and was not even allowed to wash. Long walks were also prescribed. Even on his deathbed he was still correcting the proofs for *Winter Journey*. His works are songs of love and pain. In 'My Dream', an early prose piece, Schubert wrote: 'For long, long years I sang songs. When I would sing of love, it turned to pain. And again, when I would sing of pain, it turned to love.'[3]

Beauty is pain's complementary colour. Faced with pain, the mind imagines beauty. The mind juxtaposes what is disfigured by pain with what is unscathed. The semblance of beauty *soothes* the pain. Pain causes the mind to erect a healing – liveable – counter-world, in which everything appears in a new, seductive light: 'The tremendous tension imparted to the intellect by its desire to oppose and counter pain makes him see everything he now beholds in a new light: and the unspeakable stimulus which any new light imparts to things is often sufficiently powerful to defy all temptation to self-destruction and to make continuing to live seem to the sufferer extremely desirable.'[4] Pain enlivens the imagination. For Nietzsche, art is a 'saving sorceress with the power to heal' who can spirit away what is unbearable and terrifying about existence.[5]

Nietzsche, too, would call our society a palliative society. Our society is characterized by a withering of the sense of life. Life dwindles to a form of *comfortable survival*. Health is elevated to the status of the new goddess. Nietzsche would say that the *tragic*, the very element which affirms life amid the most extreme pain and suffering, has evaporated from life: 'The psychology of the orgiastic, as an overflowing feeling of life and strength where even pain acts as a stimulus, gave me the key to the concept of *tragic* feeling.'[6]

Society's general anaesthesia leads to the complete disappearance of the poetics of pain. Anaesthesia suppresses the aesthetics of pain. In the palliative society, we forget altogether how pain can be narrated, and even sung. We forget how to give it a language, to translate it into a narration, to drape it in the semblance of beauty, even to outwit it. Today, pain is entirely cut off from the aesthetic imagination. Because it has been made a matter of medicine alone, it has been deprived of language. Analgesia pre-empts the operation of narrative and the imagination, and puts them to sleep. Permanent anaesthesia leads to mental numbness. Pain is stopped before it can bring about a narrative. Within the palliative society, pain is not a navigable river, not a narrative flow leading man down to the sea, but a *dead-end street*.

The French writer Michel Butor speaks of a crisis of literature. He thinks that literature is no longer capable of creating a new language: 'For ten or twenty years almost nothing has happened in literature. There has been a deluge of publications, but no intellectual movement. The cause for this is a crisis in communication. The new means of communication are admirable, but they produce an enormous noise.'[7] The noise of communication perpetuates the hell of the same. It prevents something altogether different, something incomparable or unprecedented, from happening. The hell of the same is a palliative comfort zone. Pain is driven out of it because it disturbs the circulation of communication, which must be accelerated. Communication is fastest where the same meets the same. It is accelerated by the *Like*. Pain, by contrast, counteracts it. It creates an *inclination to fall silent*. This inclination is what would allow for something altogether different to occur.

We are not prepared to expose ourselves to pain. Pain is the midwife of the new, of the wholly other. The negativity of pain disrupts the same. In the palliative society, as the hell of the same, a language of pain, a poetics of pain, is impossible. It only permits a *prose of pleasure*, a writing in the sun.

The Dialectic of Pain

The mind is pain. It is only through pain that the mind reaches new insights, higher forms of knowledge and consciousness. The mind, Hegel says, is characterized by the capacity 'to preserve itself in contradiction and, therefore, in pain'.[1] On its formative path, the mind ends up in contradiction with itself.* It becomes divided. It is pained by this division, this contradiction, but this pain ensures that the mind keeps on *forming itself.* Formation presupposes the negativity of pain. The mind overcomes the painful contradiction by developing into a higher form. Pain is the motor of the dialectical formation of the mind. It *transforms* the mind. Transformations are tied to pain. Without pain, the mind remains identical with itself. The formative path is a *via dolorosa*: 'The Other, the negative, contradiction, rupture, thus belongs to the nature of mind. In this rupture lies the possibility of *pain.*

Pain has therefore not come to the mind from outside, as people imagined when they posed the question about the way in which pain came into the world.'[2] The mind 'only wins its truth by finding its feet in its absolute disruption'. Its power is revealed by it 'looking the negative in the face and lingering with it'. The positive 'that avoids looking at the negative',[3] by contrast, withers and becomes 'dead being'.[4] Only the negativity of pain keeps the mind alive. *Pain is life*.

Without pain, it is impossible to produce that kind of *knowledge* which radically breaks with the past. *Experience* [Erfahrung] in an emphatic sense also pre-supposes the negativity of pain. Experience is a painful process of transformation that contains an element of suffering, of undergoing something. Experience differs in this way from an experienced event [Erlebnis], which does not bring about a change in one's state; it amuses rather than transforms. Radical change is brought about only by pain. In the palliative society, we just have more of the same. We travel everywhere without *experiencing* anything. We take note of everything without gaining *knowledge* of it. *Information* leads neither to experience nor to knowledge. It lacks the *negativity of transformation*.

The negativity of pain is constitutive of thought. Pain is what distinguishes thinking from calculating, from artificial intelligence. Intelligence means *choosing between* (*inter-legere*). It is a faculty of discrimination, and thus it does not go beyond what is already there. It is not capable of bringing forth what is *wholly other*. It differs in this way from the *mind*. Pain makes thinking more profound. There is no such thing as profound computing. What constitutes the *profundity* of thinking? As opposed to

39

computing, thinking brings forth an altogether different perspective on the world, even *another world*. Only what is living, what is capable of experiencing pain, can think. This is precisely what artificial intelligence lacks: 'We are no thinking frogs, no objectifying and registering devices with frozen innards – we must constantly give birth to our thoughts out of our pain and maternally endow them with all that we have of blood, heart, fire, pleasure, passion, agony, conscience, fate, and disaster.'[5] An artificial intelligence is nothing but a computing machine. It may well be capable of learning, even of *deep learning*, but it is incapable of experience. *Only pain can transform intelligence into mind.* There will be no *pain algorithms*. 'Only great pain, that long, slow pain that takes its time,' Nietzsche says, 'is the liberator of the spirit.' It 'forces us philosophers to descend into our ultimate depths and put aside all trust, everything good-natured, veiling, mild, average – things in which formerly we may have found our humanity.'[6]

Unlike pain, health is non-dialectical. The palliative society, which declares health to be the highest value, is trapped in the hell of the same. It lacks the dialectical force of transformation. At one point, Nietzsche speaks of a higher form of health, one that incorporates pain: 'And as far as my long infirmity is concerned, isn't it the case that I am unspeakably more indebted to it than I am to my health? I owe a *higher* health to it, a health that becomes stronger from everything that does not kill it off! *I owe my philosophy to it as well.*'[7] Even his *revaluation of all values* Nietzsche derives from pain. Pain shakes up the habitual relations between meanings, and forces the mind into a radical change in perspective that shows everything in a new light. As opposed to pleasure, pain triggers

40

processes of reflection. It gives the mind a 'dialectical *clarity par excellence*'. It makes the mind *more perceptive*. It opens up a whole new way of seeing: 'In my case, a complete lucidity and serenity of spirit is compatible not only with the most extreme physiological weakness but even with extreme feelings of pain. In those agonies that go along with a continuous pain during the arduous vomiting of mucus, I possessed a dialectical clarity *par excellence* and thought through things for which, in a healthier condition, I would not be enough of a mountaineer, not clever enough. . . . I have it at my disposal, this knack for *shifting perspectives*: which is the only reason why I was able to undertake a *revaluation of values* in the first place.'[8]

Instead of lingering with negativity, the palliative society desperately flees from it. In holding on to positivity, it reproduces the same. This 'persisting in the *same* forms' rests on algophobia. The 'eternally creative, as *that which must eternally destroy*', is 'bound to pain'. Pain 'compels the creator to feel previous things as untenable, misshapen, worthy of renunciation, as ugly'.[9] Without pain, there is thus also no revolution, no departure from the old, no history.

The Ontology of Pain

Pain gives of its healing power where we least expect it.
Martin Heidegger

SINGABLE REMNANT – the outline
of him, who through
the sicklescript broke through unvoiced,
apart, at the snowplace.
*Paul Celan**

In a marginal note to Jünger's *On Pain*, Heidegger writes: 'A treatise "On Pain" which never and nowhere treats of pain itself; does not ask after its essence; never confronts the questionability of the question because it cannot at all be affected by the secret of pain, as a consequence of its decisively reifying attitude towards pain.'[1] Jünger takes it for granted that everyone knows what pain is. He is interested above all in our relation to pain: 'Pain is one of the keys to unlock man's innermost being as well as the world. Whenever one approaches the points where man proves himself to be equal or superior to pain, one gains access to the sources of his power and the secret hidden behind his dominion. Tell me your relation to pain, and I will tell you who you are!'[2] On this, Heidegger remarks: 'Tell me your relation to being, if you even have an inkling of it, and I will tell you how, and whether, you will "concern" yourself with "pain", or whether you will be able to pursue it in your thinking.'[3]

Heidegger's seemingly ironic reply to Jünger possesses a philosophical core. Heidegger wants to approach the question of pain from the side of being. Only through being can we access the 'essence', the 'secret', of pain. Heidegger would even say: *being is pain*. By this, however, he would not mean that human existence is particularly painful. Rather, Heidegger has in mind an *ontology of pain*. He wants to get to the 'essence' of pain by way of being: 'Immeasurable suffering creeps and rages over the earth. The flood of suffering rises ever higher. But the essence of pain is concealed. . . . Everywhere we are assailed by innumerable and measureless suffering. We, however, are unpained, not brought into the ownership of the essence of pain.'[4]

Heidegger's thinking takes as its point of departure the ontological difference between being and beings. Beings owe their manifestness, their comprehensibility, to being. The disclosure of being is necessary for a comprehending comportment towards beings. Before directing my attention at an object, I already *find myself* in a *pre-reflexively* disclosed world. Heidegger points out

43

that moods [Stimmungen] possess a world-disclosing power. The world as pre-reflexively disclosed by a mood precedes intentionality, the aiming at an object: '*The mood has already disclosed, in every case, Being-in-the-world as a whole, and makes it possible first of all to direct oneself towards something.*'[5] This interest in phenomena such as 'moods' reveals that Heidegger's thinking is concerned with what is *non-available*. We cannot avail ourselves of the pre-reflexively disclosed world. We are *thrown* into it; we are at its mercy and de-*termined* [be-*stimmt*] by it.* A mood, after all, is something that *comes over* us, something we cannot appropriate.

In the later Heidegger, being takes on a mystical meaning as the 'source' of beings.[6] Being does not create beings, but it lets each become what it *is*. Humans also owe their existence to being: 'Humans are at-tuned [ge-stimmt] to what de-termines [be-stimmt] their essence. In this de-termining, humans are touched and called forth by a voice [Stimme] that peals all the more purely the more it silently reverberates through what speaks.'[7] That silent voice which de-*termines* and suf-*fuses* [durch-stimmt] human Dasein evades any form of availability. It comes from *somewhere else*, from what is *altogether other*. Thinking is the pain, the *passion for the secret* that 'withdraws, halts in its withdrawal'.[8]

Heidegger considers language to be a *gift*. Human beings speak [sprechen] by *according with* it [ihr *entsprechen*]. The ontological difference between being and beings also determines language: 'An "is" arises where the word breaks up. To break up here means that the sounding word returns into soundlessness, back to whence it was granted: into the ringing of stillness. . . .'[9] The 'is' marks

44

the non-available origin of language, which – as *stillness* – cannot be captured by the sounding word. Only when the word breaks do we hear the stillness. Only poetry lets us hear that soundless stillness, that *remainder that can be sung* and that silently breaks through the sounding word. Poetry returns what is readable to the *unreadable* from where it arose. The *seam* that ties the readable to what can be sung *is painful*. Heidegger's 'seamstress'[10] guards pain. Pain is the tear through which *stillness*, the *non-available outside*, breaks into thinking. The remainder that can be sung *rhymes with pain*.

Pain is the fundamental mood of human finitude. Heidegger thinks pain from the perspective of death: 'Pain is death on a small scale – death is pain on a large scale.'[11] Heidegger's thinking traces that area of being 'in which pain and death and love belong together'.[12] It is the *unavailability of the other*, in particular, that keeps love, in the sense of Eros, alive. Eros is the *desire for an other* who escapes my grasp. Death is not simply the end of life, conceived of as a biological process. Rather, it is a particular *way of being*. As the 'mystery of being', it reaches into life. It is 'the shrine of the nothing, namely of that which in all respects is never some mere *being*, but nonetheless essences, even as the mystery of *being* itself'.[13] Death indicates that human beings are related to the non-available, to the altogether other that does not come from death.

Being only becomes perceptible under the condition of the pain of 'pure nearness that can stand the distance'.[14] Pain makes the human being receptive for the non-available, which gives him a hold and refuge. Pain *bears* human Dasein. This is how it differs from pleasure. It is not a temporary condition that can be removed. Rather, it constitutes the *gravity* of human Dasein: 'But the more joyful the joy, the more pure the sadness slumbering within it. The deeper the sadness, the more summoning the joy resting within it. Sadness and joy play into each other. The play itself which attunes the two by letting the remote be near and the near be remote is *pain*. This is why both, highest joy and deepest sadness, are painful each in its way. But pain so touches the spirit of mortals that the spirit receives its gravity from pain. That gravity keeps mortals with all their wavering at rest in their being. The spirit [muot] which answers to pain, the spirit attuned by pain and to pain, is melancholy [Schwermut].'[15]

Concealment is the fundamental figure in Heidegger's thinking. 'Concealment' is an essential part of truth, understood as 'unconcealment'. Being, as 'clearing', is surrounded by a dark forest. The earth represents what is 'essentially self-secluding' and evades all attempts at grasping it: 'Earth shatters every attempt to penetrate it. It turns every merely calculational intrusion into an act of destruction. Though such destruction may be accompanied by the appearance of mastery and progress in the form of the technological-scientific objectification of nature, this mastery remains, nonetheless, an impotence of the will. The earth is openly illuminated as itself only where it is apprehended and preserved as the essentially undisclosable, as that which withdraws from every disclosure, in other words, keeps itself constantly closed up. . . . The earth is the essentially self-secluding.'[16] If the earth is treated as a resource to be opened up, it is already destroyed, no matter how 'sustainable' our approach may be, because as earth it is 'essentially undisclosable'. *Saving the earth* presupposes establishing an altogether different

46

relation to it. We need to treat it *with care*. A crucial part of taking care of it is the experience of unavailability. Such care allows the earth to retain its otherness and strangeness. *Treating something with care demands distance.*

Today, the terrestrial order, the order of the earth, is coming to an end. It is being succeeded by the digital order. Heidegger was the last thinker of the terrestrial order. Death and pain do not belong to the digital order. They represent *disturbances*. Mourning and longing are also suspicious. The *pain of the nearness of distance* is alien to the digital order. Distance is inscribed into nearness. The digital order transforms nearness into the absence of distance, so that it is no longer painful. Under the compulsion of availability, everything is rendered accessible and consumable. The *digital habitus* is: everything must be available at once. The telos of the digital order is total availability. This order lacks the 'slowness of the hesitant shyness in the face of what cannot be done'.[17]

Within the terrestrial order, the mysterious is essential. The watchword of the digital order, by contrast, is *transparency*. The digital order eliminates anything that could be concealed. The digital order also makes language transparent, that is, available, by reifying it into information. Information has no hidden *reverse side*. When transformed into data, the world becomes transparent. Algorithms and artificial intelligence also make human behaviour transparent, that is, calculable and controllable. The soul of the digital order is dataism, data totalitarianism. In place of narration, it substitutes addition. 'Digital' means numerical. The numerical is more transparent, more available, than the narrative.

Today, non-availability just means a temporary absence

of availability. A world consisting exclusively of available things can only be consumed. But the world is more than the sum total of what is available. The available world loses its *aura*, its *scent*. It does not permit any *lingering*. Non-availability also characterizes the otherness of the other, its *alterity*. It protects the other against its being demeaned by becoming an object of consumption. Without 'primordial distance', the other is not a *thou*.[18] He is reified into an *it*. The other is not *appealed to* in his otherness, but instead appropriated.*

Pain makes possible *another kind of visibility*. It is a mode of sensation that we are in the process of losing. The digital order is *anaesthetic*; it abolishes certain forms of temporality and perception. Heidegger would have said that the digital order leads to the forgetfulness of being. Impatience, the compulsion of immediate access, leads to the disappearance of what is enduring and slow. The enduring and slow is not deprived of anything, because it does not lack anything. It does not indicate a process that can be accelerated. Rather, it possesses its own temporality, its own reality, its *own scent*. What is available *does not have a scent*. The enduring and slow *hesitates* in withdrawing [*zögert* im Entzug]. It is a *laggard* [*Nachzügler*], a *lagging light* [*Nachleuchter*]. Lateness is its pace. '*At once*', by contrast, is the temporality of the digital.

The mental attitude that shows *patience* and is prepared *to wait* is eroding. It provides access to a reality which we are losing amid the compulsion of total availability. A waiting which remains patient within the enduring and slow exhibits a specific kind of intentionality. It is an attitude that resigns itself to the non-available. It is not a case of *waiting for* but of *waiting in*. It is characterized

48

by an in-sistence. This attitude follows the contours of the non-available. Renunciation is the fundamental trait of *intentionless waiting*. Renunciation *gives*. It makes us receptive to the non-available. It is opposed to consumption. The 'mournful bearing of the need to renounce and to give away' is, Heidegger says, a 'receiving'.[19] Pain is not a subjective sensation pointing to a lack of something but a reception, even the reception of being. *Pain is a gift.*

The Ethics of Pain

ErnstJünger's reflections on pain are determined throughout by the idea of discipline. He sees modern media, such as photography and film, in the context of a disciplinary technique whose purpose is to render the human being insensitive to pain. Only superficially do they serve the purposes of entertainment. In the background, they serve to discipline our seeing: 'Special forms of discipline are hidden behind the entertaining aspect of communications technologies, such as radio and film.'[1] 'The photograph', Jünger writes, 'stands outside of the zone of sensitivity'. It is characterized by a cold gaze. Thus, a camera 'captures a man at the moment an explosion tears him apart'.[2] It embodies the disciplined seeing of the human eye. Photography is 'an expression of our peculiarly cruel way of seeing'.[3] Film expresses 'an exceptional degree of cold cruelty'.* The spectator is desensitized by the 'synchronicity of events, where images of luxurious comfort are interrupted by images of a catastrophe simultaneously devastating a part of the globe'.[4] The silence of the audience is 'by far more abstract and crueller than the wild rage one can witness in the southern arenas, where, in the bullfight, for instance, remnants of the Ancient Games are still preserved'.[5]

The cultural practices of our time do not involve this disciplining of our ways of seeing. Digital media are not disciplinary media. We do not live in a disciplinary society but in a consumer society, in which everything is consumable. Even our relation to images of violence is pornographic. In films and computer games we indulge in *violence porn*. This turns even killing into a painless affair. The pornographic images of violence have the effect of an analgesic. They make us insensitive to the pain of others.

The excess of images depicting pain and violence in the mass media and on the internet likewise force us to adopt the passivity and indifference of the silent spectator. So numerous are these images that we cannot cognitively come to terms with them. They impose themselves on our perception. They no longer express the moral imperative described by Susan Sontag: 'The image says: put an end to this, intervene, act.'[6] The deluge of images of violence and pain decouples perception from action because acting presupposes intense attention, a *shock*. Our attention is so fragmented that such shock is impossible.

The common anthropological assumption that humans take voyeuristic pleasure in the pain of others does not suffice to explain the rapid decline of our capacity for empathy. Behind the loss of empathy is a particularly profound event: *the disappearance of the other*. The palliative society eliminates the other as pain. The other is reified into an object. *The other as an object does not cause pain.*

In a pandemic, the suffering of others becomes even more remote. It dissolves into 'numbers of cases'. People die alone in intensive care units, without being afforded any human affection. Nearness means infection. 'Social distancing' contributes to the loss of empathy. It turns into mental distancing. The other becomes no more than a potential carrier of the virus, someone from whom one must keep one's distance. 'Social distancing', in turn, becomes a form of behaviour that is held in high regard.

Today, we are utterly dominated by the ego – even dazed, intoxicated by it. The increasingly strong narcissistic ego, in confronting the other, mainly meets itself when it meets the other. Digital media also tends to promote the disappearance of the other. By making the other *available*, it diminishes the *resistance of the other*. We find it increasingly difficult to perceive the otherness of the other. The other deprived of his or her otherness can only be consumed.

A sensibility for the other presupposes an '*exposure*' that 'offer[s] itself even in suffering'.[7] This is pain.[8] Without this *primordial pain*, the ego rears its head again, its *for-oneself*, and reifies the other into an object. The other is withdrawn from the grasp of the ego only with the ego's pain of being exposed. This pain, as an ethical, *meta*-physical pain, precedes the kind of pain which I experience as *mine*. It is a pain *towards the other*, an original being exposed that is more passive than any passivity of the ego. The pain of exposure, which also precedes compassion, renders a *comfortable return to oneself*, the *pleasure in oneself*, impossible.

'*Being able to*' – that is the modal verb of the ego as the subject of performance. Consuming, enjoying and experiencing are synonyms for '*being able to*'. Making '*being able to*' the absolute standard destroys the other, who, in their unavailability, reveal themselves precisely in the pain of '*being-able-not-to-be-able*'. Love, as an emphatic relationship to another, 'invades and wounds us'.[9] Love as consumption, by contrast, does not involve injury, is free of all pain. The subject of performance, with its '*being able to*', is invulnerable as such because it is *resilient*. Being receptive to the other presupposes vulnerability. The painful *wound* is a *primordial opening to the other*.

Elias Canetti speaks of the 'naked soul' that is defenceless against the other, and thus *vulnerable*. On account of this state of the soul, I experience *restlessness* in the face of the other. It makes indifference towards the other impossible: 'He thinks of his pathetic contacts and of his inner life, also of the fact that in his old age he is more powerfully afflicted by love than ever, not at all preoccupied with his own death but all the more incessantly with the death of his loved ones; he realizes that he is becoming less capable of being "objective" toward those close to him and never indifferent, that he despises everything that is not breathing, feeling, and insight. But he also realizes that he does not want to see others, that every new person agitates him to the core of his being, that he cannot defend himself against this tumult either by aversion or by contempt, that he is utterly at the mercy of everyone, defenseless (though the other doesn't notice it), that he can find no rest on account of this other, no sleep, no dreams, no breath – . . . .'[10] The nakedness of the soul results in fear for others. It is this fear for others that teaches me who I am: 'Only in fear am I completely myself – why is that? Have I been raised to be fearful? I recognize myself only in fear. Once it has been overcome, it turns into hope. But it is fear for others. The people I have loved were those for whose life I feared.'[11]

Today, we are in the process of altogether losing this nakedness of soul, exposure, the pain towards the other. The skin of our soul has, as it were, formed a callus, rendering us completely insensitive and unreceptive in the face of the other. Our digital bubbles also increasingly shield us from the other. A *definite fear for others* gives way to a diffuse fear for oneself. Without pain towards the other we do not have access to the pain of the other.

The Last Man

Francis Fukuyama's book *The End of History* is not just a one-sided encomium to liberal democracy in the context of the demise of communism. In fact, it is pervaded by ambivalence. The last part of the book, titled 'The Last Man', states that liberal democracy produces the kind of palliative society symbolized by Nietzsche's 'last human being'.* This is a society of permanent anaesthetization: 'A bit of poison once in a while; that makes for pleasant dreams. And much poison at the end, for a pleasant death. ... One has one's little pleasure for the day and one's little pleasure for the night: but one honors health. "We invented happiness" say the last human beings, and they blink.'[1]

Fukuyama proceeds from the anthropological thesis that megalothymia, a striving after superiority, fame and honour that takes on heroic proportions, is essential to the human being. It is also the driving force of history. But in liberal democracy this megalothymia is tempered by isothymia, that is, by a striving for equality with others, and a more intense striving after convenience and security. Liberal democracy thus leads to the emergence of the last man: 'to the extent that liberal democracy is successful at purging *megalothymia* from life and substituting for it rational consumption, we will become last men'.[2]

But the emergence of the last man is not, as Fukuyama claims, necessarily bound up with liberal democracy. Rather, the last man is a proper phenomenon of *modernity*. The last man does not necessarily prefer the liberal system. He is, for instance, quite happy to live under a totalitarian regime. Today, China is just as populated by last men as the US. Everywhere heroism gives way to hedonism. It is for this reason that Jünger turns decidedly against modernity. In *On Pain*, he invokes the end of the age of the last man: 'The *breadth* of people partaking of goods and pleasures is a sign of prosperity. . . . Here one senses the dream-like, painless, and oddly agitated ease that fills the air like a narcotic. . . . The individual is greeted by a wealth of conveniences . . . The potential for conflict is thereby avoided. What is more, a quality of pure convenience is still an integral part of the fabulous expansion of technical means – it all seems designed to light up, warm, move, entertain, and deliver streams of gold. The prophecy of the Last Man has found rapid fulfillment. It is accurate – except for the assertion that the Last Man lives longest. His age already lies behind us.'[3]

Looking forward to the year 2000, Jünger writes: 'The Last Man, as Nietzsche prophesied, is already history, and even if we have not yet reached the year 2000, it seems certain it will look entirely different than depicted in Bellamy's utopia.'[4] Jünger's reference is to the pain-free society of Edward Bellamy's utopian novel *Looking Backward: 2000–1887*. We must presumably conclude that Jünger's prediction was mistaken, for the twenty-first century is precisely the age of the last man. The heroic age between the two world wars, invoked by Jünger, was only a brief episode. The palliative society of the twenty-first century dismisses any kind of heroic demeanour.

Fukuyama's prediction has also turned out to have been mistaken. History did not end with the triumph of liberalism. In particular, there is currently widespread support for right-wing populism and autocracy. As a survival society, the palliative society does not necessarily depend on liberal democracy. In the face of the pandemic, we are drifting towards a regime of biopolitical surveillance. Western liberalism seems to be failing to rise to the challenge posed by the virus, and we will soon realize that in the fight against the pandemic the focus must be on the behaviour of each individual. But the biopolitical surveillance of the individual does not sit well with the principles of liberalism. Under the influence of the hygienic dispositif, the society of survival will find that it is forced to give up those liberal principles.

The regime of digital surveillance, taking on proto-totalitarian traits by now, is already undermining the liberal idea of freedom. The individual has been transformed into a data set and exploited for profit. Capitalism has developed into surveillance capitalism.[5] Surveillance generates capital. Digital platforms subject us to constant surveillance and manipulate our behaviour. Our thoughts, feelings and intentions are read and exploited.

The internet of things extends this surveillance into real life in the physical world. Wearables expose our bodies to commercial exploitation. We are like marionettes being directed by algorithmic strings. The psychopolitical instrument of Big Data renders human behaviour predictable and controllable. Digital psychopolitics creates a crisis of freedom.[6]

In connection with the census in West Germany in the 1980s, there were widespread protests against the collection of data. The suspicion was that behind the census lurked a surveillance state that threatened liberal freedom. From today's perspective, the information requested was rather innocent – educational qualifications, profession, religion – and yet even schoolchildren took to the streets. Today, we voluntarily give away even the most intimate personal data. We expose ourselves not because we are compelled to do so but out of an inner need. We allow all aspects of ourselves to be scrutinized. Domination becomes total the moment it coincides with freedom. What we are witnessing here is a dialectic of freedom. The freedom of limitless communication turns into total surveillance.

Why should this enormous apparatus of digital surveillance, already implemented and meeting with little resistance, stop short of the virus? Rather, the pandemic will soon dissolve the inhibition which has hitherto prevented the biopolitical expansion of digital surveillance down to the level of the individual. According to Naomi Klein, the moment of shock is the perfect opportunity to establish a new system of domination. The shock of the pandemic will ultimately lead to the triumph of a global biopolitical surveillance regime that permits access to the body. Only digital biopolitics can inoculate capitalism against the pandemic. Digital biopolitics closes a systemic gap. But the biopolitical regime of surveillance spells the end of liberalism. Liberalism will prove to have been merely a historical episode.

The last man is not a partisan of liberal democracy. For the last man, comfort is a higher value than freedom. The illiberalism of digital psychopolitics does not disturb him. His mania for health is such that he is constantly monitoring himself. He erects an *internal dictatorship*, a *regime of control inside himself*. Where an internal dictatorship confronts biopolitical surveillance, it does not perceive it as oppressive, for this surveillance comes in the name of health. Within the biopolitical regime, then, the last man feels free. Domination and freedom again coincide.

Nietzsche already saw the pain-averse, palliative society coming: "'It will come, one day, that hour that will envelop you in a golden cloud where there is no pain: where the soul has the enjoyment of its own weariness and, happy in a patient game with its own patience, is like the waves of a lake which, reflecting the colours of an evening sky on a quiet summer's day, lap and lap against the bank and then are still again – without end, without aim, without satiation, without desire – all repose that rejoices in change, all ebbing back and flooding forward with the pulsebeat of nature." This is how all invalids feel and speak: but if they do attain to that hour there arrives, after brief enjoyment, boredom.'[7] Fukuyama entertains the possibility that man, out of unbearable boredom, might set history in motion again, that the society of last men might give way to a society of bestial first men, a society of uninhibited megalothymia.[8] But there will be no such return to the past. An altogether different future awaits us, the post-humanist age in which the last man and his boredom will have been overcome.

In *The Hedonistic Imperative*, the transhumanist David Pearce declares that the future will be pain-free: 'Over the next thousand years or so, the biological substrates of suffering will be eradicated completely. "Physical" and "mental" pain alike are destined to disappear into evolutionary history.'[9] The pain of love, those 'soul-destroying cruelties of traditional modes of love', will also be overcome.[10] The aim of transhumanism is 'a sublime and all-pervasive happiness'.[11] Transhumanism leaves behind even the last man, because, as Pearce might say, he is still all too human. He is beset with boredom. Transhumanism believes that even boredom can be overcome through biotechnology: 'Whatever humanity's contemporary failures of imagination, within a few generations the experience of boredom will be neurophysiologically impossible. "Against boredom even the gods struggle in vain", said Nietzsche; but he failed to anticipate biotechnology.'[12]

The pain-free life of permanent happiness is not a human life. Life which tracks down and drives out its own negativity cancels itself out. Death and pain belong together. In pain, death is anticipated. If you seek to remove all pain, you will have also to abolish death. But life without death and pain is not human life; it is undead life. In order to survive, humans are abolishing themselves. They may succeed in becoming immortal, but only *at the expense of life itself*.

NOTES

Algophobia

1 Ernst Jünger, *On Pain*, Candor: Telos Press, 2008, p. 32.

2 See Chantal Mouffe, *Agonistics: Thinking the World Politically*, London: Verso, 2013.

3 See Barbara Ehrenreich, *Smile or Die: How Positive Thinking Fooled America and the World*, London: Granta, 2010.

4 See Edgar Cabanas and Eva Illouz, *Manufacturing Happy Citizens: How the Science and Industry of Happiness Control our Lives*, Cambridge: Polity, 2019.*

5 David B. Morris, *The Culture of Pain*, Berkeley: University of California Press, 1991, p. 71.

6 Marcus Woeller, 'Gefälligkeiten machen sich bezahlt', *Die Welt*, 18 May 2019.

7 See Byung-Chul Han, *Saving Beauty*, Cambridge: Polity, 2017, p. 2.

8 Astrid Mania, 'Alles wird Pop', *Süddeutsche Zeitung*, 8/9 February 2020.

9 Theodor W. Adorno, *Aesthetic Theory*, London: Continuum, 2002, p. 183.

10 Ibid., p. 331.

11 Martin Heidegger, *Parmenides*, Bloomington: Indiana University Press, 1992, pp. 166f.

12 Adorno, *Aesthetic Theory*, p. 331.*

The Compulsion of Happiness

1 Michel Foucault, *Discipline and Punish: The Birth of the Prison*, New York: Vintage, 1995, p. 8.*

2 Jünger, *On Pain*, p. 44.

3 Ibid., p. 41.

4 Ibid., p. 44 (transl. modified).

5 Aldo Palazzeschi, 'Counterpain: Futurist Manifesto', in *The Manifestos of Aldo Palazzeschi*, New York: Bordighera Press, 2019, pp. 21–39; here p. 24 (transl. amended).

6 Jünger, *On Pain*, p. 40.

7 Ibid., p. 41 (transl. modified).

8 Ehrenreich, *Smile or Die*, London: Picador, 2010, pp. 179f.

9 Theodor W. Adorno, *Negative Dialectics*, London: Routledge, 1973, pp. 17f. (transl. amended).

10 Friedrich Nietzsche, *The Gay Science*, Cambridge: Cambridge University Press, 2001, p. 192.

11 Friedrich Nietzsche, *Nachgelassene Fragmente 1880–1882*, Kritische Studienausgabe, vol. 9, Munich: Deutscher Taschenbuch Verlag, 1999, p. 641.

Survival

1 See Giorgio Agamben, *Homo Sacer: Sovereign Power and Bare Life*, Stanford: Stanford University Press, 1998.

2 See Byung-Chul Han, *Capitalism and the Death Drive*, Cambridge: Polity, 2021.

The Meaningless of Pain

1 Ivan Illich, *Medical Nemesis: The Expropriation of Health*, New York: Pantheon, 1976, p. 145.

2 Jean Starobinski, *Kleine Geschichte des Körpergefühls*, Frankfurt am Main: Fischer Verlag, 1991, p. 118.

3 Helmut Lethen, '"Schmerz hat keinerlei Bedeutung" (Paul Valéry) Oder: Gibt es Ereignisse, die den Kulturwissenschaften den Atem verschlagen?', in *Wo ist Kultur? Perspektiven der Kulturanalyse*, ed. Thomas Forrer and Angelika Linke, Zurich: vdf Verlag, 2014, pp. 37–56; here p. 42.

4 Paul Valéry, *Monsieur Teste*, Princeton: Princeton University Press, 1973, p. 20.

5 Teresa of Ávila, *The Collected Works of St. Teresa of Avila*, vol. 1 (The Book of Her Life/Spiritual Testimonies/ Soliloquies), Washington, DC: The Institute of Carmelite Studies, 1976, p. 252.

6 Starobinski, *Kleine Geschichte des Körpergefühls*, p. 136.

7 Walter Benjamin, 'Storytelling and Healing', in *Thought Figures*, in *Selected Writings*, vol. 2, part 2, Cambridge, MA: Harvard University Press, 1999, pp. 724–5; here p. 724.

8 Ibid., pp. 724f.

9 Walter Benjamin, 'Outline of the Psychophysical Problem', in *Selected Writings*, vol. 1, Cambridge, MA: Harvard University Press, 1996, pp. 393–401; here p. 397.

10 Starobinski, *Kleine Geschichte des Körpergefühls*, pp. 137f.

11 See Odo Marquard, 'Die modernen Menschen als Prinzessinnen auf der Erbse', in *Skepsis und Zustimmung: Philosophische Studien*, Stuttgart: Reclam, 1994, pp. 99–109.

The Cunning of Pain

1 Jünger, *On Pain*, p. 36 (transl. modified).

2 Ibid., p. 40.

3 Andrew H. Knoll, *Life on a Young Planet*, Princeton: Princeton University Press, 2003, p. 41.
4 Jünger, *On Pain*, p. 20.
5 Ibid., p. 19f.
6 Viktor von Weizsäcker, 'Die Schmerzen', in *Der Arzt und der Kranke: Stücke einer medizinischen Anthropologie*, Gesammelte Schriften, vol. 5, Frankfurt am Main: Suhrkamp, 1987, pp. 27–4; here p. 27.

Pain as Truth

1 Von Weizsäcker, 'Die Schmerzen', p. 35.
2 Ibid.
3 Ibid.
4 Alain Badiou with Nicolas Truong, *In Praise of Love*, London: Serpent's Tail, 2012, p. 6.
5 Von Weizsäcker, 'Die Schmerzen', p. 34.
6 Illich, *Medical Nemesis*, p. 152.

The Poetics of Pain

1 Max Brod and Franz Kafka, *Eine Freundschaft: Briefwechsel*, vol. 2, Frankfurt am Main: Fischer, 1989, pp. 377f.
2 Stefan Zweig, 'Der Snob, der den Tod besiegte: Marcel Prousts tragischer Lebenslauf', *Die Zeit*, 21 January 1954.
3 Franz Schubert, 'My Dream', quoted after Maynard Solomon, 'Franz Schubert's "My Dream"', *American Imago*, vol. 38, no. 2 (Summer 1981), pp. 137–54; here p. 138.*
4 Friedrich Nietzsche, *Daybreak: Thoughts on the Prejudices of Morality*, Cambridge: Cambridge University Press, 1997, p. 114.
5 Friedrich Nietzsche, *The Birth of Tragedy*, in *The Birth of Tragedy and Other Writings*, Cambridge: Cambridge University Press, 1999, pp. 1–116; here p. 40.

6 Friedrich Nietzsche, *Twilight of the Idols*, Cambridge: Cambridge University Press, 2005, p. 228.

7 Interview with Michel Butor in *Die Zeit*, 12 July 2012.

The Dialectic of Pain

1 Georg Friedrich Wilhelm Hegel, *The Philosophy of Mind*, Oxford: Clarendon, 2007, p. 16.

2 Ibid., p. 16.

3 Georg Friedrich Wilhelm Hegel, *The Phenomenology of Spirit*, Cambridge: Cambridge University Press, 2018, p. 21.

4 Ibid., p. 158.

5 Nietzsche, *The Gay Science*, p. 6.

6 Ibid.

7 Friedrich Nietzsche, *Nietzsche Contra Wagner: From the Files of a Psychologist*, in *The Anti-Christ, Ecce Homo, Twilight of the Idols and Other Writings*, Cambridge: Cambridge University Press, 2005, pp. 263–82; here p. 280.

8 Friedrich Nietzsche, *Nachgelassene Fragmente 1887–1889*, Kritische Studienausgabe, vol. 13, Munich: Deutscher Taschenbuch Verlag, 1999, p. 630.

9 Friedrich Nietzsche, *Unpublished Fragments (Spring 1885–Spring 1886)*, in *The Complete Works of Friedrich Nietzsche*, vol. 16, Stanford: Stanford University Press, 2019, p. 354.

The Ontology of Pain

1 Martin Heidegger, *Zu Ernst Jünger*, Gesamtausgabe, vol. 90, Frankfurt am Main: Vittorio Klostermann, 2004, p. 436.

2 Jünger, *On Pain*, p. 32.

3 Heidegger, *Zu Ernst Jünger*, p. 439.

4 Martin Heidegger, 'The Danger', in *Bremen and Freiburg Lectures: Insight Into That Which Is and Basic Principles*

of Thinking, Indiana: Indiana University Press, 2012, pp. 44–63; here p. 54.

5 Martin Heidegger, *Being and Time*, Oxford: Basil Blackwell, 1962, p. 176.

6 Martin Heidegger, *What is Called Thinking*, New York: Harper and Row, 1968, p. 11.

7 Martin Heidegger, *The Principle of Reason*, Bloomington: Indiana University Press, 1991, p. 50.

8 Martin Heidegger, 'The Nature of Language', in *On the Way to Language*, New York: Harper and Row, 1971, pp. 57–108; here p. 66.

9 Ibid., p. 108.

10 Martin Heidegger, *Country Path Conversations*, Bloomington: Indiana University Press, 2010, p. 102.

11 Martin Heidegger, 'Zum Ereignis-Denken', Gesamtausgabe, vol. 73.1, Frankfurt am Main: Vittorio Klostermann, 2013, p. 735.

12 Martin Heidegger, 'Why Poets?', in *Off the Beaten Track*, Cambridge: Cambridge University Press, 2002, pp. 200–41; here p. 205.

13 Martin Heidegger, 'The Thing', in *Bremen and Freiburg Lectures*, pp. 5–22; here p. 17 (emphasis added, BCH) (transl. amended).

14 Martin Heidegger, *Erläuterungen zu Hölderlins Dichtung*, Gesamtausgabe, vol. 3, Frankfurt am Main: Vittorio Klostermann, 1981, p. 146.

15 Martin Heidegger, 'Words', in *On the Way to Language*, pp. 139–56; here p. 153.

16 Martin Heidegger, 'The Origin of the Work of Art', in *Off the Beaten Track*, pp. 1–56; here p. 25.

17 Martin Heidegger, *Hölderlins Hymne 'Andenken'*, Gesamtausgabe, vol. 52, Frankfurt am Main: Vittorio Klostermann, 1982, p. 128.

18 See Martin Buber, *Urdistanz und Beziehung*, Heidelberg: Lambert Schneider, 1978.*

19 Martin Heidegger, *Aus der Erfahrung des Denkens 1910–1976*, Gesamtausgabe, vol. 13, Frankfurt am Main: Vittorio Klostermann, 1983, p. 94.

The Ethics of Pain

1 Jünger, *On Pain*, p. 57.

2 Ibid., p. 55.

3 Ibid., p. 56.

4 Ibid., p. 57 (transl. amended).

5 Ibid. (transl. modified).

6 See Susan Sontag, *Das Leiden anderer betrachten*, Munich: Hanser, 2003 (cover text).*

7 Emanuel Levinas, *Otherwise than Being, or Beyond Essence*, Dordrecht: Springer, 1991, p. 15.

8 See ibid., p. 55.

9 Emanuel Levinas, *Time and the Other*, Pittsburgh: Duquesne University Press, 1987, p. 89.

10 Elias Canetti, *The Secret Heart of the Clock: Notes, Aphorisms, Fragments 1973–1985*, New York: Farrar, Strauss, Giroux, 1989, pp. 135f.

11 Ibid., p. 30.

The Last Man

1 Friedrich Nietzsche, *Thus Spoke Zarathustra*, Cambridge: Cambridge University Press, 2006, p. 10.

2 Francis Fukuyama, *The End of History and the Last Man*, New York: The Free Press, 1992, p. 314.

3 Jünger, *On Pain*, p. 38.

4 Ibid., p. 36.

5 See Shoshana Zuboff, *The Age of Surveillance Capitalism: The Fight for a Human Future at the New Frontier of Power*, London: Profile Books, 2019.

6 See Byung-Chul Han, *Psychopolitics: Neoliberalism and New Technologies of Power*, London: Verso, 2017.

7 Friedrich Nietzsche, *Human, All Too Human*, Cambridge: Cambridge University Press, 1996, pp. 291f. (transl. modified).

8 See Fukuyama, *The End of History*, pp. 329f.

9 David Pearce, *The Hedonistic Imperative*, chapter 0.1 (all chapters can be accessed at https://www.hedweb.com/hedethic/tabconhi.htm).

10 Ibid., chapter 1.8.

11 Ibid., chapter 0.1.

12 Ibid., chapter. 4.7.

TRANSLATOR'S NOTES

Page vi, epigraph: Walter Benjamin, 'Outline of the Psychophysical Problem', in *Selected Writings*, vol. 1, Cambridge, MA: Harvard University Press, 1996, pp. 393–401; here p. 397.

Page 16: See Byung-Chul Han, *The Scent of Time: A Philosophical Essay on the Art of Lingering*, Cambridge: Polity, 2017, chapter 1; esp. p. 2.

Page 16: 'Vermögen' means both 'capacity' and 'wealth' or 'asset'.

Page 21: The German translation of *Monsieur Teste* has 'entsetzliches Ding' – terrible thing – where the English translation gives 'object'.

Page 32: 'Anti-body' translates Han's neologism 'Gegen-Körper', meaning a body that opposes us. This should not be confused with the term 'antibody' in the sense of the proteins formed in the body as an immunological response to antigens.

Page 38: 'Formative path' translates 'Bildungsweg' which could equally be translated as 'education'. The same double meaning applies to 'forming', 'formation' below.

Page 42, epigraphs: Martin Heidegger, 'The Thinker as Poet', in *Poetry, Language, Thought*, New York: HarperCollins, 1971, p. 7. Paul Celan, 'Singable Remnant' (from *Breathturn*), in *Paul Celan: Selections*, Berkeley: University of California Press, 2005, p. 99.

Page 44: The German for 'mood', 'Stimmung', forms part of a range of expressions, such as 'bestimmen' (to define or to determine), abstimmen/stimmen (to coordinate or to tune), and 'etwas stimmt nicht' (to be not quite right). 'Stimme' is 'voice' (e.g. 'die Stimme der Mehrheit' = 'the voice of the majority').

Page 48: The German term 'angerufen' is a nod to Heidegger's *Being and Time*, where 'Anruf' is variably translated as 'appeal' (in the Macquarrie and Robinson translation of 1962) or 'summons' (Stambaugh translation, Albany: SUNY, 1996). See esp. §§ 54–60.

Page 50: My translation. The English edition leaves out this passage.

Page 55: I follow here the translation of Nietzsche's 'letzter Mensch' as the 'last human being' in the edition of *Thus Spoke Zarathustra* quoted below. Fukuyama's 'last man' is, of course, Nietzsche's 'letzter Mensch', and that expression is also used in the German translation of Fukuyama's text.

Page 61, note 4: The term 'posttraumatic growth' was coined in a clinical context by Lawrence G. Calhoun and Richard

G. Tedeschi. See their *Handbook of Posttraumatic Growth: Theory and Practice*, New York: Psychology Press, 2014.

Page 62, note 12: The full passage from Adorno runs: 'Ultimately, aesthetic comportment is to be defined as the capacity to shudder, as if goose bumps were the first aesthetic image. What later came to be called subjectivity, freeing itself from the blind anxiety of the shudder, is at the same time the shudder's own development; life in the subject is nothing but what shudders, the reaction to the total spell that transcends the spell. Consciousness without shudder is reified consciousness. That shudder in which subjectivity stirs without yet being subjectivity is the act of being touched by the other.'

Page 62, note 1: The German text omits the passage between 'should not all this' and 'yet the fact remains that'. The German translation of Foucault allows for this possibility, while it would make the English translation ungrammatical. I have therefore included the passage.

Page 64, note 3: This article contains the full text of the short prose piece on pp. 137f.

Page 67, note 18: I follow the original German title. The essay has been translated as 'Distance and Relation', *Hibbert Journal*, vol. 49 (1951), 105–13, and can also be found in *The Martin Buber Reader*, ed. A. D. Biemann, New York: Palgrave Macmillan, 2002, pp. 206–13.

Page 67, note 6: My translation, as the formulation is not to be found in the original English edition: Susan Sontag, *Regarding the Pain of Others*, London: Hamish Hamilton, 2003.